Harry Stratford Caldecott

Spoils

Studies in Shakespeare

Harry Stratford Caldecott

Spoils
Studies in Shakespeare

ISBN/EAN: 9783337242251

Printed in Europe, USA, Canada, Australia, Japan

Cover: Foto ©Thomas Meinert / pixelio.de

More available books at **www.hansebooks.com**

S P O I L S

STUDIES IN SHAKESPEARE.

BY

HARRY S. CALDECOTT, F.R.G.S.

REVISED AND ENLARGED.

Arts and Sciences hunt after their works; human counsels after their ends; and all natural things hunt either after their food to preserve them, or after their pleasures and delights to perfect them (for all hunting is for the sake of either prey or pleasure): and this too by methods expert and sagacious.

> " The savage lioness the wolf pursues,
> The wolf the kid, the kid the cytisus."
> *De Augmentis*

PRELIMINARY REMARKS.

THERE have been, admittedly, mountains of rubbish written about Shakespeare. He has (according to Mr. Saintsbury, his latest critic and expositor) been the subject of commentatorial folly to an extent which dwarfs the expense of that folly on any other single subject. One especial form of folly has been to treat Shakespeare as, if not exactly an inspired idiot, at any rate a mainly tentative if not purely unconscious artist, much of whose work is only not bad as art, while most, if not all, of it was originally produced with a minimum of artistic consciousness and design[1]—and, I may add, with a minimum of literary preparation, and a tag-rag equipment of knowledge, comparable only to the motley of a juggler or a court fool. The business of the critic, therefore, is much more to shovel away the rubbish of his predecessors than to attempt any accummulation of his own. In the meantime certain writers have boldly put forward the theory that Shakespeare was not Shakespeare at all. The newest form of "folly," in fact, is to deny that Shakespeare wrote the plays and poems so long attributed to him—and not only to deny that Shakespeare wrote them, but to assert that his great co-temporary, Francis Bacon, did. This hypothesis—strange and startling as it may seem—is, if not proved, at least supported by many curious and ingenious arguments. Many people have been convinced of its validity, and declare that for them it has thrown fresh beauty, grandeur, and meaning on the plays, and cleared up many doubts and difficulties of criticism, which have so far defied solution.

[1] Saintsbury, "Elizabethan Literature," 1887.

Others, on the contrary, have been stirred to an exhibition of petulancy, which is always childish and often spiteful.

Shakespeare's works are amongst the most precious heritages of the world. What does it matter whether they were written by Francis Bacon or William Shakespeare? Shakespeare himself is almost a mythical being. The little that is actually known about him and his doings is hardly creditable, much less admirable. The truth is that men too often allow their judgments to be obscured by the pleasing illusions of sentiment. All that we really know of Shakspere[1] is that he was baptized on the 24th of April, 1564, at Stratford-on-Avon. His parents belonged to the lower middle class, and were connected with small farmers and farm-labourers on the one side, and with petty tradesmen on the other. Nothing is known of his youth and education ; but it was a constant tradition of the literary men of his own and the immediately succeeding generation that he had little school-learning.[2] Before he was nineteen he was married, at the end of 1582, to Anne Hathaway, who was seven years his senior. Their first child, Susannah, was baptized six months later. In 1585, at the age of 20-1, he is supposed to have gone up to London, and to have been connected with the theatres in some humble capacity. He became an actor, but acquired no fame in that capacity. He accumulated money, however, as Alleyn and other actors and stage-managers did. He appears to have been "prudent" in the ordinary way, to have bought property, sold malt, pursued petty debtors ; and in 1616 he died, unwept, unhonoured, and unsung. Some years after his death his plays were collected in the First Folio of 1623. Many of these plays had been greatly altered and augmented from the editions published in Shakspere's life-time. Many plays saw light for the first time in the Folio. In the entire number of thirty-seven plays which are usually regarded as Shakespeare's, there are only fourteen of which, in what may be called their completed state or ultimate form, we possess impressions published in his life-

---

[1] The Stratford man always signed himself "Shakspere." The author is invariably spelt "Shakespeare."

[2] Saintsbury.

tim e, together with four others of which, in an immature and imperfect state, we have such impressions. Of one other, " Othello," we have also an edition, printed, indeed, after the author's death, but apparently from another manuscript than that used for the First Folio. For the remaining eighteen plays our oldest and only authority is that edition.[1] In view of these facts, the question was raised many years ago by Mr. W. H. Smith, in his historical letter to Lord Elles-mere : *Who but the author himself could have exercised this power of discrimination ?* And the question remains un-answered to this day. It is quite clear that Shakspere had no hand in the compilation of the First Folio. He had died seven years before — died in obscurity in a country village, leaving a will, it is true, but making no refer-ence to any literary works — appointing no literary executors — leaving no library of books, no collection of correspon-dence, no manuscripts, not even the scrap of a letter.

On the other hand, in 1623, Francis Bacon—aided by Ben Jonson and many other friends—was busy collecting, correcting, and publishing his works. The " De Augmentis " was published in the same year as the famous Folio. In 1626 Bacon died, acknowledged to be the greatest and most eminent man of his age—described by Ben Jonson, in his review of the more famous names of his own and the preceding age, from Sir Thomas More to Sir Philip Sidney, Hooker, Essex, and Raleigh, as without a rival at the head of the company as the man who had " fulfilled all numbers " and " stood as the mark and *acme* of our language." " No man," he says, " ever spoke more neatly, more pressly, or suffered less emptiness, less idle-ness, in what he uttered. . . . His hearers could not cough or look aside from him without loss. He commanded when he spoke, and had his judges angry and pleased at his devotion . . . the fear of every man that heard him was that he should make an end. . . . His speech was nobly censorious when he could spare and pass by a jest."

The contention that Bacon wrote the plays is set forth at

[1] Craik, " The English of Shakespeare."

length by Judge Holmes in a learned and judicial work entitled "The Authorship of Shakespeare's Plays." Other
writers have discussed the problem from various points of view,
and with various success. The literary guides, however, upon
whom we usually rely in matters of this kind are almost
unanimous in denouncing the suggestion as a piece of folly—
madness, drunkenness—something so crass and stupid that
there is no fitting word to describe it. Professor Elze, Dr.
Furnivall, Mr. Saintsbury, all the Shakespearian critics who
have condescended to notice the discussion, fling a stone at it,
and pass on to shovel away or add to the rubbish-heap of
commentary on this inscrutable subject of William Shakespeare and his works. "As for Shakespeare-Bacon theories,
and that kind of folly," says Dr. Saintsbury, "they are
scarcely worthy even of mention." This is the contemptuous
style. "The idea of Lord Bacon's having written Shakespeare's plays," says Dr. Furnivall, "can be entertained only
by folk who know nothing whatever of either writer, or are
crackt, or who enjoy the paradox or joke." This is the angry
style. And so they all ring the changes on all the terms of
contempt and abuse they can command, until the chorus
becomes a little monotonous, and one would like to hear a
little argument and not quite so much vituperation.

Dr. Nichol, Professor of English Literature in the University
of Glasgow, is more conciliatory. He says:[1] "Lord Bacon
did not write Shakespeare's plays; but there is something
startling in the like magnificence of speech in which they find
voice for sentiments, often as nearly identical when they anti-
cipate as when they contravene the manners of thought and
standards of action that prevail in our country in our age.
They are similar in their respect for rank and dignity, in their
belief in royal right divine, in their contempt for the *vulgus
mutabile*, depreciation of the merely commercial, and exaltation
of a military spirit; above all, in their view of the duty of
Englishmen to knit together the forces and extend the bounds
of—

[1] "Francis Bacon : His Life and Philosophy," i., p. 78.

" 'This royal throne of kings, this sceptred isle,
This earth of majesty, this seat of Mars,
This fortress built by Nature for herself
Against infection and the hand of war,
This happy breed of men, this little world,
This precious stone set in the silver sea.'

" The above and numerous other passages show that neither the statesman nor the poet had, for good or evil, more share than any other Elizabethan of our recent, sometimes quixotic, cosmopolitanism."

Everywhere the writings of the one author throw light on those of the other. Dr. Nichol, commenting on Bacon's "Essay on Judicature," quotes the passage in which the duties of a judge are defined, namely, "*jus dicere* and not *jus dare*— to interpret law and not to make or give law," etc. And: " Therefore it is a happy thing in a State when Kings and States do often consult with judges ; and again, when judges do often consult with the King and State," etc. And again : " Let judges also remember that Solomon's throne was supported by lions on both sides ; let them be lions, but under the throne." The Professor comments : " This solution of the problem revolved by his contemporary in ' Measure for Measure,' and ' The Merchant of Venice,' *the relation of the letter to the spirit of the law*, is another aspect of the same practical philosophy that we have seen running through Bacon's thought and pervading his practice."

Throughout, the works of the one receive illumination by mutual annotation with those of the other. In their intellectual march they walk in step; in their sympathies, antipathies, aspirations, they are as one. In the higher reaches of their spirit, alike, they were

" Before the starry threshold of Jove's court."

Of the one as of the other it is equally true to say—as Dr. Nichol says of Bacon: " In mass, in variety, in scope, his genius is the greatest among men who have played a part at once in widening the bounds of the kingdom of thought and in fencing the bulwarks of their country."

And yet so irrational are men that when it is suggested—
and the more plausible the grounds the more offensive it seems
to be—that this man of "unequalled powers with unequalled
will," wrote or inspired the plays attributed to the shadowy
personality of the other, the only reply that most English men
of letters have is an angry taunt, an impotent gibe, or a simious
grin. These gentlemen, in fact, having (as was long since said
of them)[1] erected themselves into the condition, as it were, of
guardians and trustees of Shakespeare, they have remained
impervious to the most obvious difficulties of their situation.
For a long time they would have it that Shakespeare was a
mere dunce in book-learning—that he was alike ignorant of
that "popish language, Latin," as of all modern languages,
except English. Then it was a shock to have it demonstrated
that Shakespeare was not only learned in all languages, but
also in all sciences—botany, medicine, law, music, and the fine
arts generally, which could never have been picked up either
in the sheep-market of Stratford-on-Avon or the mews of
London. Driven from these positions—admitting now that
myriad-minded Shakespeare was learned in books as well as in
Nature, these guardians and trustees refuse to ask themselves
—or to permit others to ask—where did he get it from?
Directly this fatal question is put the records are huddled
away, and you are told that it is impertinent to ask questions.
The practice is certainly inconvenient, but this is an inquisitive
and cross-examining age. In the words of the "Recorder":[2]
"Schollers are pryed into of late, and are found to bee busye
fellowes, disturbers of the peace. Ile say no more, gesse at my
meaning, I smel a ratt."

There is no need here to attempt to add to the argument in
favour of Bacon's claims. Mr. Holmes, Mr. Donnelly, Mr.
Appleton Morgan, Mrs. Pott, Mr. R. M. Theobald, M.A., and
others, have said pretty well as much as can be said at present.
Whether, however, Bacon wrote the plays or not, his mind and
Shakespeare's appear to have run in singularly similar grooves.

---

[1] "The Dramatic Character of Sir J. Falstaff," by M. Morgann, 1825.

[2] "Returne from Parnassus," 1606.

In the ensuing essays I have endeavoured to illustrate this thesis. Similar treatment of other plays would reveal the same phenomenon. And yet, although Lord Bacon must have been well acquainted with Shakespeare, it is singular that, whilst he, in his acknowledged works, refers to most of the leading writers of his age, he never refers to, or quotes from, Shakespeare, and, but for one circumstance, might, so far as we are aware, never have heard of him. The Shakespearian quidnuncs—the Furnivalls, *et hoc genus omne*—were very much *nonplussed* a few years ago by the discovery by Mr. John Bruce of certain documents in the library at Northumberland House, somewhat mutilated, singed, and incomplete, but bearing indisputable evidence of some mysterious relationship between Bacon and Shakespeare. The manuscripts belong to about the year 1597. Indorsed on the outside leaf of " A Conference of Pleasure," being a Device by Bacon, there is a list of other manuscripts which formerly lay with it. This list includes, among other things, " Orations at Graie's Inn Revels, by Mr. Fr. Bacon "; " Essays by the same "; " Richard the Second"; " Richard the Third." These latter, Mr. Spedding (Bacon's editor) admits refer to the Shakespeare plays of those names. The outside leaf is scrawled over eight or nine times with the name " William Shakespeare." It also has the long dog-Latin word, *honorificabilitudinitatibus*, which is introduced in " Love's Labour Lost " (Act V., sc. i., l. 45), and the line,

" *Revealing day through every cranny peeps*,"

from " Lucrece."

It would seem that the plays of " Richard the Second " and " Richard the Third " had been torn out from the packet in the general work of destruction of the manuscripts of the dramas ; but by some oversight the tell-tale outer sheet had escaped observation. Here, at least, Bacon and Shakespeare—so far as external evidence goes—are brought very near together ; and it is Shakespeare that we find in Bacon's house, not Bacon in Shakespeare's. The incident is curious, and encourages Shakespearian students to hope that further manuscripts may yet turn up throwing further light on the mystery of the plays.

Indeed, in the year 1885 Mr. Macray, M.A., F.S.A., discovered in the Bodleian Library the long-lost manuscripts of two comedies, called respectively the "Pilgrimage to Parnassus" and the "Return from Parnassus," forming the first and second parts of a trilogy of dramas, known as the "Parnassus Plays." The third part, entituled "The Return from Parnassus; or, The Scourge of Simony," was twice printed in the year 1606. No one knows who wrote these plays. They contain direct and pointed references to Bacon's works, as well as to Shakespeare's plays. Shakespeare's name is introduced ironically—his poems and plays are claimed by the writer (in the character of *Gullio*) as belonging to him—and there are good reasons for believing that the plays were written by the author of the Shakespearian drama, and that the writer was not William Shakespeare. These comedies are an enigma to Shakesperian students. If, however, Dr. Abbot will apply to them his philological test, he will find they are Shakespearian; and if Mr. Moulton will apply to them his laws of art criticism, and especially his doctrine of "Central Ideas," he will find that the central idea of the first play is *Stupido*, a canting Puritan; of the second *William Shakespeare*, called ironically "Sweet Mr. Shakespeare;" and of the third, *Immerito*, an ignorant country fellow, whose father has purchased for him the living belonging to Sir Raderick, father of the impecunious scholar, Amoretto. And if anyone bring his common-sense to bear upon these comedies, he will find that they are full of bitter complaints of the consideration and wealth poured upon the ignorant play-actors, and of the neglect with which the poets and dramatists of the day were treated. A full discussion of these plays, however, would lead us too far astray. It is sufficient to indicate that, until the critics take up different standing-ground, they will probably never understand them.

Other indications are not wanting that we may expect any day to have some startling piece of evidence thrust upon our unwilling ears. The *Athenæum*, for instance, of the 16th May, 1891, published a paragraph to the effect that—

"The *Genealogist* for April contains a few brief remarks on two important and hitherto unnoticed State Papers in the Public Record Office, which Mr. James Greenstreet has recently drawn attention to, as bearing upon the oft-vexed question of the authorship of the plays printed as Shakespeare's. The documents alluded to have evidently suggested very strongly to the mind of their discoverer that many of these plays, though published under the name of Shakespeare, were not actually written by him, but by William Stanley, Earl of Derby, and that this earl, and not Lord Southampton, was Shakespeare's real patron and benefactor. And here it should be observed in what close relationship to the crown the nobleman in question stood, his brother and predecessor having been regarded by some as the possible successor of Queen Elizabeth in preference to the Scotch king."

The *Genealogist* has either published a silly *canard*, which the staid *Athenæum* has endorsed; or it has published a fact of the most extraordinary interest to the literary world. It would, of course, be premature to pass any opinion on the subject here. Indeed, I pass no opinion of any kind upon anything, unless it be to say that, so far as I can judge, the stone-throwers to whom I have referred are living in glass houses of a very fragile nature; and that a little more temperateness would be more becoming the scholarship of England than has so far characterized the utterances of the very mixed and confused tongues of the recognised Shakesperian oracles.

THE delineation of the character of Cæsar as given by Shakespeare in the great play called after that " famous man,"[1] has
always been a stumbling-block and an offence to the critics.

We are accustomed to regard Cæsar as he is described by
Antony:

> "Thou art the ruins of the noblest man
> That ever lived in the tide of times."[2]

But this is not the picture presented by Shakespeare.

M. Stapfer says :[3] " The character of Cæsar offers a comparatively ungrateful subject with which to begin a psychological study of the Roman tragedies ; not, indeed, that it is
wanting in interest when Shakespeare's meaning is fathomed,
but because it is strange and unexpected and perplexingly unlike the ordinary idea we fashion to ourselves of the Roman
hero ; the first impression it leaves on the mind is that of a
vague surprise and disappointment."

M. Mézières also complains that Shakespeare has given us
" a conventional Cæsar, very different to that of Plutarch . . .
He never tells us of the lofty thoughts with which, to the very
last, the mind of the master of the world was occupied, nor
mentions the new conquests that his genius was preparing
when he was struck down by the swords of the assassins."

Mr. Moulton, too, in his study of the character of Cæsar is
puzzled and perplexed. He says :[4] " The character of Cæsar

---

[1] " Richard III.," Act III., sc. i.   [2] "Julius Cæsar," Act III., sc. i., l. 257.
[3] " Shakespeare and Classical Antiquity," p. 321.
[4] " Shakespeare as a Dramatic Artist," p. 176.

1

is one of the most difficult in Shakespeare. Under the influence of some of his speeches we find ourselves in the presence of one of the master spirits of mankind ; other scenes in which he plays a leading part breathe nothing but the feeblest vacillation and weakness." And he sums up Shakespeare's conception of Cæsar as follows : " He is the consummate type of the practical : emphatically the public man, complete in all the greatness that belongs to action. On the other hand, the knowledge of self produced by self-contemplation is wanting, and so when he comes to consider the relation of his individual self to the state, he vacillates with the vacillation of a strong man moving amongst men of whose greater intellectual subtlety he is dimly conscious. . . ."[1]

And M. Stapfer asks :[2] " Why, then, did Shakespeare deliberately set to work to disparage his hero ? For, whether right or wrong, it is evidently the result of choice on his part ; and it is impossible to ascribe to mere negligence a contrast so disproportionate as that existing between the Cæsar who makes his appearance in a few short and rapid scenes, and the grand ideal Shakespeare himself had of him, which ideal he well knew was shared in by all his audience, and would continue to be held by them in spite of everything."

The reply seems to be that Shakespeare never had any " grand ideal "—that is to say, not any transcendental ideal— of Cæsar, but that he had read the life of Cæsar in the same practical light as Bacon had done. In this view, a short summary of Bacon's Essay ("Imago civilis Julii Cæsaris "), and a brief comparison of it, and of some other references made by Bacon to Cæsar, with the play will prove interesting.

(1) Shakespeare, M. Stapfer says, was " fully aware of the hero's historical importance."[3] Shakespeare realized " clearly enough that it was no insignificant man that fell."[4] This is quite true. And it is also true of Bacon.

Bacon grants that Cæsar had "greatness of mind in a very high degree," but he immediately adds, " yet such as aspired

---

[1] "Shakespeare as a Dramatic Artist," p. 181.
[2] "Shakespeare and Classical Antiquity," p. 325.   [3] *Ibid.*, p. 320.
[4] *Ibid.*, p. 325.

more after personal aggrandizement than merit towards the
public. For he referred everything to himself and was the
true and perfect centre of all his own actions."

Again : " And assuredly in his private wishes he cared more
for power than reputation. He sought reputation and fame
not for themselves, but as instruments of power. By natural
impulse, therefore, and not by any moral guiding, he aspired·
to the supreme authority, and aspired rather to possess it than
to be thought worthy of it—a thing which gave him favour·
with the people, who had no dignity of their own ; but with
the nobles and great persons, who wished also to preserve their
own dignity, procured him the reputation of covetousness and·
boldness."

("The people, who had no dignity of their own." Is not
this the very essence of Shakespeare's conception of "the·
people" in all the plays ?)

That is to say (according to Bacon), Cæsar was a popular
idol, but persons of keener insight recognised the bold and
covetous man, who referred everything to himself, and was the
true and perfect centre of his own actions.

"Nature ever presents two sides, one for Heraclitus and
one for Democritus." The honourable and simple-minded
Brutus, in the play, reflects the enlightened view of Cæsar's
character and aims ; whilst the dissolute and popular Antony
is an exponent of the opposite side. The opinions of these two
men must be read in the light of their respective characters and
careers. And notwithstanding that Shakespeare put language of
the greatest reverence for Cæsar's character in the mouth of
Antony, we shall find reason to believe that he, personally,
sympathized with the more severe judgment of Brutus.

(2) Bacon says that Cæsar referred everything to himself,
and was the true and perfect centre of all his own actions. In
his essay "Of Wisdom for a Man's Self," he expresses his
censure on such a character. " And certainly," he says, " men
that are great lovers of themselves waste the public. . . .[1] It is ·,

---

[1] The sentence left out in the text reads as follows : "Divide with reason
between self-love and society ; and be so true to thyself as thou be not false to ·

a poor centre of a man's actions, HIMSELF. It is right earth. For that only stands fast upon its own centre; whereas, all things that have affinity with the heavens move upon the centre of another, which they benefit." "But," he says again, " the corrupter sort of politics, that have not their minds instituted and established in the true apprehension of duties, and the contemplation of good in the universality, *refer all things to themselves as if they were the world's centre, and that the concurrence of all lines should touch in them and their fortunes;* never caring in all tempest what becomes of the ship, so they may retire and save themselves in the cockboat of their own fortune."

Bacon probably had in his mind, at the time of writing this Essay, the character of Cæsar, concerning whom he used the same language as of a man who "referred everything to himself, and was the true and perfect centre of all his own actions." Now compare with this the following striking passage in the play (Act III., sc. i., l. 59), in which Cæsar speaks of himself:

> " I could be well moved if I were you ;
> If I could pray to move, prayers would move me :
> But I am constant as the northern star,
> Of whose true-fix'd and resting quality
> There is no fellow in the firmament.
> The skies are painted with unnumber'd sparks,
> They are all fire and every one doth shine,
> And there's but one in all doth hold his place :
> So in the world ; 'tis furnish'd well with men,
> And men are flesh and blood, and apprehensive ;
> Yet in the number I do know but one
> That unassailable holds on his rank,
> Unshaked of motion.
> Hence ! wilt thou lift up Olympus ?"

Bacon's commentary upon this self-estimate of Cæsar's was simply this : " It is a poor centre of a man's actions, HIMSELF. It is right earth." And the astronomical illustration is used

---

others, especially to thy king and country." Compare this with the well-known sentiment in " Hamlet " :

> " Unto thine own self be true,
> And it must follow as the night the day
> Thou canst not then be false to any man."

alike in both authors. Cæsar likens himself to the polar star, around which all things move and circle. And the self-centred man is likened by Bacon to the earth, "which only stands fast upon his own centre."

(3) M. Mézières complained, in the passage quoted above, that Shakespeare never tells us of the lofty thoughts with which to the very last the mind of the master of the world was occupied, nor mentions the new conquests that his genius was preparing when he was struck down by the swords of the assassins. But this, assuredly, is a mistake.

According to Shakespeare the "lofty thoughts" in Cæsar's mind were concerned with the consolidation of his own power as king, and the conquests he dreamt of were the destruction of the remaining liberties of the Roman people.

This is Brutus's justification for joining the conspiracy.

The question Brutus was debating with himself was what action should be taken in view of the dangerous height to which Cæsar had advanced. He knew that Cæsar was a "great lover of himself," and he knew that such men "*waste the public.*" Brutus had no personal animus against Cæsar; but in the interest of "the general"—the public—he considered that he would be acting a patriotic part in destroying the tyrant before he had time to perfect his schemes. Whatever one's personal predilections may be, we must see the marked contrast of character presented by the dramatist in the delineation of the motives actuating Cæsar and Brutus respectively. Cæsar was as the "northern star," fixed and moving on its own centre. Brutus, on the other hand, had that "affinity with the heavens" which "move upon the centre of another"—the public weal—"which they benefit."

In this light read the speech of Brutus (Act II., sc. i., l. 10) :

> " It must be by his death : and, for my part,
> I know no personal cause to spurn at him,
> But for the general. He would be crowned :—
> *   *   *   *   *
> Crown him ? That ;—
> And then, I grant, we put a sting in him,
> That at his will he may do danger with.
> The abuse of greatness is, when it disjoins

> Remorse from power : and, to speak truth of Cæsar,
> I know not when his affections sway'd
> More than his reason."

Compare Bacon :

" At last," he says, " whether satiated with power or cor-
rupted by flattery, he aspired likewise to the external emblems
thereof (real power)—the name of king and the crown, which
turned to his destruction.   The sovereignty was the mark he
aimed at even from his youth . . . but he made himself a way
to the sovereignty in a strange order.

" First, by means of a power popular and seditious, after-
wards by a power military and imperatorial.   He broke the
force and authority of the senate ; he overthrew the power of
Crassus and Pompey.   He gave largesses to the people, cor-
rupted the courts of justice, put in seditious tribunes, secretly
favoured Catiline and his conspirators, banished Cicero, upon
whose cause the authority of the senate turned, and a number
of the like arts ; but most of all by the conjunction of Crassus
and Pompey, first with one another and then with himself.
He then consolidated his military authority, and so obliged
and bound to himself by private benefits all persons who had
any power, that there was no danger of any combination being
formed to oppose his designs before he should openly invade
the commonwealth."

(Schlegel says the following verse from Euripides was fre-
quently in the mouth of Cæsar :

" For a kingdom, it is worth while to commit injustice, but in
other cases it is well to be just "—which he quoted with the
intention of making bad use of it.)

Thus we have, presented to us by Bacon, a man bold,
covetous, and unscrupulous, employing corruption, sedition,
violence, to further his ends, and meanwhile wearing a mask
of apparent frankness and innocency.   And Shakespeare represents Brutus as mistrusting Cæsar. He feared his ambition. He
knew he would scruple at nothing to accomplish his personal
ends.   The two conceptions of Cæsar's character agree
perfectly.

(4) " He put on the appearance," says Bacon, " of modesty

but to serve a turn." This is the point of Cæsar's action in pretending to refuse the crown. Brutus *knew* that Cæsar "would be crown'd"; and he debated with himself "how that might change his nature — there's the question." Cæsar, however, artfully contrived to deceive the people as to his intentions and true ambition. And in this light—the light that Bacon throws on Cæsar's character—read the story related by Casca: "If the tag-rag people did not clap him and hiss him, according as he pleased and displeased them, as they use to do the players in the theatre, I am no true man. . . . Before he fell down, when he perceived the common herd was glad he refused the crown, he plucked me ope his doublet, and offered them his throat to cut. . . . When he came to himself again, he said, if he had done or said anything amiss, he desired their worships to think it was his infirmity" (Act I., sc. ii.).

He put on the appearance (as Bacon says he did) of modesty but to serve a turn ; he merely acted a part before the people, cringing to the masters he despised and was bent upon subduing to his own will.

(5) " His friends," says Bacon, " he chose among those not distinguished for greatness, but for their pliability and usefulness ;" and so Shakespeare represents the pliable and useful Antony as the only friend of Cæsar's worth considering.

Cassius proposes that Antony should be killed together with Cæsar. "We shall find him a shrewd contriver," urges Cassius. But Brutus objects : " For he can do no more than Cæsar can when Cæsar's head is off." And Trebonius adds: "There is no fear of him. Let him not die ; for he will live, and laugh at this hereafter."

Professor Dowden describes Antony as " a man of genius, without moral fibre." A nature, in fact, agreeing with Bacon's description, " not distinguished for greatness, but for pliability and usefulness."

(6) To complete the picture of Cæsar's character (so different from the popular one), Bacon says that "in letters and learning Cæsar was *moderately* well accomplished, but it was that kind of learning which was of use in the business of life."

The play nowhere gives any idea of great culture or refinement on the part of Cæsar. Indeed, as Moulton points out, he is the type of the practical, the public man, the man of action; but amongst men of intellectual subtlety, in the supreme act of his life, he is conscious of his inferiority, and is struck with hesitancy and vacillation.

Cæsar, in fact, expressly declares his dislike and distrust of learned men. Of Cassius, he says :

> " He thinks too much ; such men are dangerous.
>
>   *   *   *   *   *
>
> He reads too much ;
> He is a great observer and he looks
> Quite through the deeds of men," etc.

The presence of the subtle and studious Cassius made Cæsar feel uncomfortable. He preferred men that were " fatter."

(7) Brutus thus sums up the opinions and feelings concerning Cæsar which were entertained by himself and those " nobles and great persons, who wished also to preserve their own dignity " : " If there be any in this assembly, any dear friend of Cæsar's, to him I say that Brutus' love to Cæsar was no less than his. If, then, that friend demand why Brutus rose against Cæsar, this is my answer: Not that I loved Cæsar less, but that I loved Rome more. Had you rather Cæsar were living, and all die slaves, than that Cæsar were dead, to live all free men ? As Cæsar loved me, I weep for him ; as he was fortunate, I rejoice at it; as he was valiant, I honour him; but as he was ambitious, I slew him. There is tears for his love ; joy for his fortune ; honour for his valour ; and death for his ambition. Who is here so base that would be a bondman ? If any, speak, for him have I offended. Who is here so rude that would not be a Roman? If any, speak, for him have I offended. Who is here so vile that will not love his country ? If any, speak, for him have I offended."

In one word : " I have saved you and your liberties by destroying the tyrant who was about to spring at the throat of Rome."

Mark the following parallels :

"There is tears for his love."—*Shakespeare*.

" In his friendship he was constant, and singularly kind and indulgent."—*Bacon*.

"Joy for his fortune."—*Shakespeare*.

" Julius Cæsar had from the beginning a fortune full of exercise, which he turned to his advantage ; for it took away his pride and braced his sinews."—*Bacon*.

"Honour for his valour."—*Shakespeare*.

"It was in the business of war that his ability was most conspicuous."—*Bacon*.

" And death for his ambition."—*Shakespeare*.

"In quest of real power . . . he aspired . . . to the name of king and the crown : which turned to his destruction."—*Bacon*.

(8) In conclusion, how does Antony meet the charges brought against Cæsar by Brutus ?

In that artful and ironical speech made by Antony over the bleeding remains of " Great Cæsar," he professes that he has come to bury, not to praise him, thereby dexterously escaping the necessity of answering the charge of " ambition."

> " Yet Brutus says he was ambitious ;
> And Brutus is an honourable man.
> *   *   *   *   *
> I speak not to disprove what Brutus spoke,
> But here I am to speak what I do know."

And so, without really meeting the charge, he passes on to gloss over the crime of which Brutus had accused Cæsar ; without seeking to remove the disapprobation of Cæsar's design upon the liberties of Rome, he still, by the magic arts of popular oratory, contrived to excite the sympathy of the people with the murdered tyrant.

> " You all did love him once, not without cause ;
> What cause withholds you then to mourn for him ?"

He then appeals to the cupidity of the crowd by referring to Cæsar's will :

> " 'Tis good you know not that you are his heirs,
> For if you should, O, what would come of it !"

It was a bitter and a fitting end that Antony should base Cæsar's claim for vengeance on the ground of the " private benefits" the people were to derive from him even in his death :

> " He hath left you all his walks,
> His private arbours, and new planted orchards,
> On this side Tyber ; he hath left them you
> And to your heirs for ever ; common pleasures,
> To walk abroad, and recreate yourselves.
> Here was a Cæsar : when comes such another ?
> 1st Cit.—Never, never ; come away !
> We'll burn his body in the holy place,
> And with the brands fire the traitors' houses.
> Take up the body."

Yes! the noble, single-hearted Brutus—"the pure champion of Roman liberty," as Schlegel calls him—was "a traitor." The destroyer of men and liberties ; the subverter of honour and justice—"Here was a Cæsar!" a man to the popular taste, "a mortal God."

(9) This is how Coleridge read the character of Shakespeare's Cæsar. The note is short, but how piercing ! He quotes (Act IV., sc. iii., l. 21, speech of Brutus) :

> " —— What, shall one of us,
> That struck the foremost man of all this world,
> But for supporting robbers, shall we now
> Contaminate our fingers with base bribes ?"

He comments :

"This seemingly strange assertion of Brutus' is unhappily verified in the present day. What is an immense army, in which the lust of plunder has quenched all the duties of the citizen, other than a horde of robbers, or differenced only as friends are from ordinary reprobate men ? *Cæsar supported, and was supported by, such as these ;* and even so Buonaparte in our days."

Shakespeare knew not Buonaparte ; but Coleridge (bearing in mind Shakespeare's character of Cæsar) recognised that they were alike—full of the lust of power, trampling down all things human and Divine to compass their own ends.

Of Cæsar, Bacon says : "For he allowed neither country, nor religion, nor services, nor kindred, nor friendship to be any hindrance or bridle to his purposes."

(10) One striking feature of the play of "Julius Cæsar" is

the part that ENVY plays as a motive-power in inducing the catastrophe. In the characters of Cæsar and Brutus, we have the antithesis of two men, one whose guiding star was Himself, whilst the other was stirred to action by consideration of the public weal. In Cassius we find a man whose mind is embittered by Envy. "*Love* and *Envy*," says Bacon, "do make a man pine, which other affections do not, because they are not so continual" (Act I., sc. ii., l. 192):

> "*Cæsar.* Let me have men about me that are fat:
> Sleek-headed men and such as sleep o' nights;
> *Yond Cassius has a lean and hungry look.*
> *He thinks too much; such men are dangerous.*
> * * * * *
> Such men as he are never at heart's ease
> Whiles they behold a greater than themselves,
> And therefore are they very dangerous."

"Envy," says Bacon, "is ever joined with the comparing of a man's self; and where there is no comparison no envy." The following further passages from the play indicate the passion of Envy, in Cassius, prompted by comparison (Act I., sc. ii., l. 135):

> "*Cassius.* He doth bestride the narrow world
> Like a Colossus, and we petty men
> Walk under his huge legs and peep about
> To find ourselves dishonourable graves."

Again (l. 152):

> "When went there by an age, since the great flood,
> But it was famed with more than with one man?
> When could they say till now, that talk'd of Rome,
> That her wide walls encompass'd but one man?"

And, again, Envy is the prompting spirit that inspired Cassius' bitter speech (l. 119):

> "He had a fever when he was in Spain,
> And when the fit was on him I did mark
> How he did shake: 'tis true this god did shake,
> His coward lips did from their colour fly,
> And that same eye, whose bend doth awe the world,
> Did lose his lustre: I did hear him groan:
> Aye, and that tongue of his, that bade the Romans
> Mark him, and write his speeches in their books,

> Alas, it cried, ' Give me some drink, Titinius,'
> As a sick girl.   Ye gods, it doth amaze me,
> A man of such a feeble temper should
> So get the start of the majestic world,
> And bear the palm alone."

In these speeches we observe that ENVY is prompted by comparison, the true test of this infirmity of human nature, according to Bacon's analysis of that passion.

(11) As for Cæsar's " audacity," Bacon says : " He was naturally very audacious."   And Shakespeare represents him as saying (Act II., sc. ii., l. 44) :

> " Danger knows full well
> That Cæsar is more dangerous than he :
> We are two lions litter'd in one day,
> And I, the elder and more terrible ;
> And Cæsar shall go forth."

(12) In Bacon's essay " Of Friendship" he writes : " With Julius Cæsar, Decimus Brutus had obtained that interest as he set him down in his testament, for heir in remainder after his nephew.   And this was the man that had power with him, to draw him forth to his death.   For when Cæsar would have discharged the Senate in regard of some ill presages, and especially a dream of Calphurnia, this man lifted him gently by the arm out of his chair, telling him he hoped he would not dismiss the Senate *till his wife had dreamt a better dream.*"

In Act II., sc. ii., l. 58 we find Shakespeare writing as follows :

> " *Deci. Brutus.* Cæsar, all hail ; good morrow, worthy Cæsar,
> I come to fetch you to the Senate-house.
>   *Cæsar.* And you are come in very happy time,
> To bear my greeting to the Senators,
> And tell them that I will not come to-day.
>   *Deci. Brutus.* Most mighty Cæsar, let me know some cause,
> Lest I be laugh'd at when I tell them so.
>   *Cæsar.* The cause is in my will ; I will not come—
> That is enough to satisfy the Senate.
> But, for your private satisfaction,
> Because I love you, I will let you know,
> Calphurnia here, my wife, stays me at home.
> She dreamt to-night she saw my statue,
> Which like a fountain with an hundred spouts
> Did run pure blood ; and many lusty Romans
> Came smiling and did bathe their hands in it."

Decius Brutus ridicules the interpretation placed upon this dream by Cæsar and Calphurnia,[1] and says :

> " When Cæsar's wife shall meet with *better dreams,*
> If Cæsar hide himself, shall they not whisper,
> Lo, ' Cæsar is afraid ' ?"

By these persuasions Brutus drew Cæsar forth to his death. (13) In Bacon's " Sylva Sylvarum," Cent. x., Ex. 940, he says :

" There was an Egyptian Soothsayer that made Antonius believe that his genius (which otherwise was brave and confident) was in the presence of Octavianus Cæsar poor and cowardly ; and therefore he advised him to absent himself (as much as he could), and remove far from him. This soothsayer was thought to be suborned by Cleopatra, to make him live in Egypt and other remote places from Rome. Howsoever, the conceit of a predominant or mastering spirit, of one man over another, is ancient and received still, even in vulgar opinion."

In the play of " Antony and Cleopatra," Shakespeare has exactly reproduced Bacon's prose (Act II., sc. iii.) :

> " *Soothsayer.* But yet hie you to Egypt again.
> *Antony.* Say to me, whose fortunes shall rise higher,
> Cæsar's or mine ?
> *Soothsayer.* Cæsar's. Therefore, O Antony, stay not by his side.
> Thy Dæmon, that's thy spirit which keeps thee, is
> Noble, courageous, high, unmatchable,
> Where Cæsar's is not. But near him thy angel
> Becomes a fear, as being overpower'd ; therefore
> Make space enough between you."

Antony exclaims :

> " I will to Egypt."

(14) Concerning the character of Cicero, Shakespeare represents him, in the words of Brutus, as one who " will never follow anything that other men begin." This recalls the circumstance that Cicero consulted the Oracle of Delphi, by

---

[1] The peculiarity of the form given to the name of Cæsar's wife in this play does not seem to have been noticed. The only form of the name known to antiquity is *Calpurnia.* And that is also the name even in North's English translation of Plutarch—Shakespeare's great authority. Mr. Senior, in his late reprint of Bacon's " Essays," at p. 99, gives the name *Calfurnia.* --CRAIK.

"what means he might rise to the greatest glory," and " the priestess bade him follow nature, and not take the opinion of the multitude for the guide of his life." Plutarch says that at first Cicero was called " a Greek and a Scholastic " at Rome, and that he rendered the Greek terms of logic and natural philosophy into the Roman language. In the play, Shakespeare brings out these scholastic tendencies of Cicero in the following passage (Act I., sc. ii.) :

> "*Cassius.* Did Cicero say anything ?
> *Casca.* Aye, he spoke *Greek*.
> *Cassius.* To what effect ?
> *Casca.* Nay, and I tell you that, I'll ne'er look you in the face again. But those that understood him smiled at one another, and shook their heads ; but for mine own part, it was *Greek* to me."

" These exquisite studies of character and history," says Mr. Wigston, " carried out to the minutest particulars by the author of the plays, are all against Shakespeare ; who is supposed to have written for the common people, and purely for pot-boiling purposes ; and what should the people care whether Cicero knew Greek or no, or whether he was a man who would not follow the leadership of others ?"

One other " touch " Shakespeare gives to the character of Cicero, showing how closely he had studied his character ; Cicero was said to be extremely vain, and we have this brought out in the passage (Act I., sc. ii.)—

> " And Cicero
> Looks with such ferret and such fiery eyes,
> As we have seen him in the Capitol,
> Being cross'd in conference by some senators."

In another passage the sceptical turn of Cicero's mind is well brought out. Cicero was what is called in these days an Agnostic, one who professed to hold nothing for certain, except the proved and established facts of science. In this respect, Bacon resembled his great forerunner. Cicero is constantly in Bacon's mind, and it has been noted that in the "De Augmentis," Cicero is cited thirty-one times, and in " An Advertisement touching an Holy War," Bacon compares his fall to Cicero's. The passage we allude to is in Act I., sc. iii., in which Casca describes the terrible portents and prodigies that were seen on the night preceding the murder of Cæsar. Cicero thereupon remarks (l. 33) :

> "Indeed, it is a strange dispos'd time :
> But men may construe things, after their fashion,
> Clean from the purpose of the things themselves "

—a sentiment which lies at the root of a great part of Bacon's own philosophy.

(15) This comparison of the play with Bacon's Essay and other references to Julius Cæsar, has, as I anticipated, brought out some striking and interesting results, which assist in removing the difficulties felt by the established Shakespearian critics, regarding the motives of the dramatist in his characterization of the great Cæsar, and some of his contemporaries. So far from the character of Cæsar offering a comparatively ungrateful subject with which to begin a psychological study of the Roman tragedies, it offers in fact a most subtle and interesting example. Bacon thoroughly appreciated the limitations of Cæsar's character. Granting him full credit for his splendid courage, penetration, energy, for his generosity, his magnanimity and his soldier-like eloquence ; he yet saw that Cæsar's was not one of those simple and elevated characters that find the spring of their activity in purely altruistic motives, but that he was largely actuated by selfish ambition, and that he was absolutely unscrupulous in the means he employed in the attainment of his ends. From this point of view, M. Mézières' dissatisfaction is removed. Cæsar's " lofty thoughts" were centred in himself, and he was dreaming of a crown and the consolidation of his authority over the Roman Empire, when he was struck down by the swords of the patriotic enthusiast, Brutus, and the envious Cassius. To Stapfer's question, " Why, then, did Shakespeare deliberately set to work to disparage his hero ?" the answer is that Bacon had measured and summed up his moral character.

(16) We find that the play (like Bacon's Essay) is distinguished by a singularly judicial spirit. Cæsar was " a famous man"; "a valiant man" ; a man "constant in friendship "; "a

fortunate man"; but, on the other hand, " an ambitious man." And this was the vice in his nature, that turned his nobility into dross. As Bacon says : " It is a poor centre of a man's actions, HIMSELF." This, is evidently the key to the play, as it is the key to Bacon's estimate of Cæsar's character. In the same judicial spirit, Bacon says of Cæsar, that he was " the most excellent spirit, *his ambition reserved*, of the world." In the play Brutus speaks of him as " the foremost man of all this world " (Act IV., sc. iii., l. 22) ; and in Bacon's "Conference of Pleasure," one of the speakers calls Cæsar " the worthiest man that ever lived."

When the matter is looked at fairly, there is really no attempt, as M. Mézières thinks, to "disparage" or belittle Cæsar. The object of the playwright, as of the philosopher, is to read Cæsar's character aright, to measure it with the square and compass of the impartial critic and to set down a true picture of the man, extenuating nothing, nor aught setting down in malice. Bacon may have taken a mistaken view of Cæsar's character. The great modern historical white-washer, Mr. Froude, may be more just in his estimate of Cæsar. This, however, is beside the point. What we want to do is to discover the point of view from which Shakespeare drew his picture. We find the critics floundering. They have no canon to guide them. Coming to the play, each with his preconceived opinion about Cæsar, they are unable to understand what Shakespeare meant by presenting so " conventional " —so " unsatisfactory "—a study of their hero. The play, however, is completely illuminated by the light thrown on it by a study of Bacon's work. The play and the essay are companion pictures, which should hang together on one wall.

(17) It is noticeable that Shakespeare's play opens with a festival in honour of Cæsar's coming " in triumph over Pompey's blood" ; that is, his victory over Metellus Scipio, and " Pompey's faction." Now, there is an old English play called " Cornelia,"[1] translated out of the French of R. Garnier by

---

[1] *Quære.* Is this the play of " Asmund and Cornelia," referred to on the outside sheet of the "Northumberland MS.," discovered by Mr. John Bruce,

Thomas Kyd, published in 1595, the action of which exactly ends at the point where Shakespeare took it up. Kyd, somehow, is curiously mixed up with Shakespeare's work. Malone (ed. by Bosw., ii. 316) attributed to Kyd the old plays of " King Lear," " Hamlet," " The Taming of the Shrew," and the " Hamlet " no longer known. The play of " Cornelia " is constructed on the old Latin plan, with the *long speeches*, the chorus, and the dumb show—exactly as Professor Arber speculates that the original " Hamlet " was constructed (Introduc. to Greene's " Menaphon," xiv.). The argument of " Cornelia " is as follows : Cornelia, the daughter of Metellus Scipio, a young Roman lady, as much accomplished with the graces of the body and the virtues of the mind as ever any was, was first married to young Crassus, who died with his father in the discomfiture of the Romans against the Parthians; afterward she took to second husband Pompey the Great, who (three years after), upon the first fires of the civil wars betwixt him and Cæsar, sent her from thence to Mitilen, there to attend the uncertain success of those affairs. And when he saw that he was vanquished at Pharsalia, returned to find her out, and carry her with him into Egypt, where his purpose was to have re-enforced a new army, and given a second assault to Cæsar.

In this voyage he was murdered by Achillus and Septimius the Roman before her eyes, and in the presence of his young son Sextus and some other Senators, his friends. After which she retired herself to Rome. And Scipio her father, being made general of those that survived after the battle, assembled new forces, and occupied the greater part of Afric, allying himself to Juba, King of Numidia. Against all whom Cæsar (after he had ordered the affairs of Egypt and the state of Rome) in the end of winter marched. And there (after many light encounters) was a fierce and furious battle given amongst them, near the walls of Tapsus ; where Scipio, seeing himself

---

in 1867, upon which the names of Francis Bacon and William Shakespeare were scribbled by some idle hand, in or about the year 1597 ? See Spedding's " Introd. Conf. of Pleasure."

subdued and his army scattered, he betook himself with some small troop to certain ships, which he caused to stay for him.

Thence he sailed toward Spain, where Pompey's faction commanded, and where a sudden tempest took him on the sea, that drove him back to Hippon, a town in Afric, at the devotion of Cæsar, where (lying at anchor) he was assailed, beaten, and assaulted by the adverse fleet ; and—for he would not fall into the hands of his so mighty enemy—he stabbed himself, and suddenly leapt overboard into the sea, and there died.

Cæsar (having finished these wars, and quietly reduced the towns and places thereabout to his obedience) returned to Rome in triumph for his victories ; where this most fair and miserable lady, having overmourned the death of her dear husband, and understanding of these cross events and hapless news of Afric, together with the piteous manner of her father's end, she took (as she had cause) occasion to redouble both her tears and lamentations, wherewith she closeth the catastrophe of this their tragedy.

(18) This play is evidently the germ out of which Shakespeare's play grew. As this fact has not been noticed before, and as the play itself is little known to general readers, I propose to give a sketch of it, by means of brief extracts, which the reader may compare, if he likes, with Shakespeare's work. The *dramatis personæ* are : M. Cicero, Philip, Decimus Brutus, M. Antony, Cornelia, C. Cassius, Julius Cæsar, *The Messenger*, and Choruses.

The first act consists of a long speech by Cicero, and some verses by the chorus. Cicero prays the gods that, if it be necessary to have a sacrifice to spare the city her liberties, he may be chosen. He is impatient of the languor of the people, and appeals to the memory of Brutus Manlius, hardy Scævola, and stout Camillus. He refers to Cæsar's personal ambition—that poison of the political atmosphere which lies at the heart of Shakespeare's drama.

> " Under a tyrant see our bastard hearts
> Lie idly sighing ; while our shameful souls
> Endure a million of base controls.
> Poison'd ambition (rooted in high minds),

'Tis thou that train'st us into all these errors :
Thy mortal covetise perverts our laws,
And tears our freedom from our franchis'd hearts.

* * * * *

Carthage and Sicily we have subdued,
And almost yoked all the world beside :
And, solely through desire of public rule,
Rome and the earth are waxen all as one :
Yet now we live despoil'd and robb'd by one
Of th' ancient freedom, wherein we were born.
And e'en that yoke, that wont to tame all others,
Is heavily return'd upon ourselves."

In the second act Cornelia pours out to Cicero her tale of grief and sorrow. Cicero endeavours to soothe her by saying that Pompey had died honourably, fighting for his country's weal. But he nevertheless suggests that the day may come when Cornelia's "grief shall turn to joy, and we have time to bury our annoy." Fortune, he says, stays not in a place, but (like the clouds) continually doth range, or like the sun that hath the night in chase. He suggests that flattering Chance, that trained Cæsar's first designs, may change her looks, and give the tyrant over—

" Leaving our city, where so long ago
Heavens did their favours lavishly bestow."

In the third act Cicero makes a long and impassioned speech, part of which I transcribe for the purpose of showing the state of feeling in Rome which led up to the assassination of Cæsar :

" Then, O world's queen ! O town that did extend
Thy conquering arms beyond the ocean,
And throng'dst thy conquests from the Lybian shores,
Down to the Scythian swift-foot fearless porters,
Thou art embas'd ; and at this instant yield'st
Thy proud neck to a miserable yoke.
Rome, thou art tam'd, and th' earth, dew'd with thy blood,
Doth laugh to see how thou art signioriz'd.
The force of heaven exceeds thy former strength :
For thou, that wont'st to tame and conquer all,
Art conquer'd now with an eternal fall.
Now shalt thou march, thy hands fast-bound behind thee,
Thy head hung down, thy cheeks with tears besprent,
Before the victor ; while thy rebel son,
With crowned front triumphing follows thee.

* * * * *

Cæsar is like a brightly burning blaze,
That fiercely burns a house already fir'd ;
And, ceaseless launching out on every side,
Consumes the more, the more you seek to quench it,
Still darting sparkles, till it find a train
To seize upon, and then it flames amain.

    *   *   *   *

But if in us be any vigour resting,
If yet our hearts retain one drop of blood,
Cæsar, thou shalt not vaunt thy conquest long,
Nor longer hold us in this servitude.

    *   *   *   *   *

Think'st thou to signiorize, or to be king
Of such a number nobler than thyself ?
Or think'st thou Romans bear such bastard hearts,
To let thy tyranny be unrevenged ?
No ; for methinks I see the shame, the grief,
The rage, the hatred, that they have conceived,
And many a Roman sword already drawn,
T' enlarge the liberty that thou usurp'st,
And thy dismembered body (stabb'd and torn),
Dragg'd through the streets, disdained to be borne.

                                                [*Exit.*"

In the fourth act we have a dialogue between Cassius and Decimus Brutus. Cassius is bewailing:

" Accursed Rome, that arm'st against thyself
A tyrant's rage, and mak'st a wretch thy king.

    *   *   *   *   *

So Rome to Cæsar yields both power and pelf,
And o'er Rome Cæsar reigns in Rome itself.
   Deci. Brutus. I swear by Heaven, the Immortal's highest
      throne,
Their temples, altars, and their images,
To see (for one) that Brutus suffer not
His ancient liberty to be repress'd.

    *   *   · *   *   *

If he determine but to reign in Rome,
Or follow Pompey but to this effect ;

    *   *   *   *   *

Then shall he see, that Brutus this day bears
The selfsame arms to be aveng'd on him ;

    *   *   *   *   *

   Cassius. In spite of Cæsar, Cassius will be free."[1]

---

[1] *Cf.* Act I., sc. iii.,
     " *Cas.* Cassius from bondage will deliver Cassius,"
et passim.

The fourth act presents to us Cæsar and Mark Antony in conference. Cæsar apostrophizes Rome, and continues :

> " Cæsar is now earth's fame and Fortune's terror,
> And Cæsar's worth hath stain'd old soldiers' praises.
>   *   *   *   *   *
> Now therefore let us triumph, Antony ;
> And rend'ring thanks to Heaven as we go,
> For bridling those that did malign our glory,
> Let's to the Capitol.
>   *Ant.* Come on, brave Cæsar,
> And crown thy head and mount thy chariot.
> Th' impatient people run along the streets,
> And in a rout against thy gates they rush,
> To see their Cæsar after dangers past,
> Made conqueror and emperor at last."

Cæsar expresses some uneasiness about the enmity he may have aroused by the blood he has been compelled to shed.

> " I joy not in the death of citizens ;
> But, through my self-will'd enemies despite
> And Romans' wrong, was I constrain'd to fight."

Antony warns Cæsar that there are conspiracies afoot for his destruction, and urges him to take steps for his own protection. Cæsar, however, true to his character, refuses to take harsh measures :

> " What, shall I slay then all that I suspect ?
>   *Ant.* Else cannot Cæsar empery endure.
>   *Cæsar.* Rather I will my life and all neglect.
> Nor labour I my vain life to assure ;
> But so to die, as dying I may live,
> And, leaving off this earthly tomb of mine,
> Ascend to heaven upon my winged deeds.
>   *   *   *   *   *
> The quiet life, that carelessly is led,
> Is not alonely happy in this world ;
> But death itself doth sometimes pleasure us.
> That death, that comes unsent for or unseen,
> And suddenly doth take us at unawares,
> Methinks is sweetest ; and, if Heaven were pleas'd,
> I could desire that I might die so well.
> The fear of evil doth afflict us more
> Than th' evil itself, though it be ne'er so sore."

In the fifth act a messenger announces to Cornelia the manner of Scipio's defeat and death, and Cornelia redoubles

" her tears and lamentations, wherewith she closeth the catastrophe of this their tragedy."

Here Shakespeare's play resumes the subject.

(19) To me, it seems that these two plays should be read
together. They are, in fact, complementary the one of the
other. It gives a fuller picture of the times and of the great
characters of Cæsar and Cicero, besides adding to the com-
pleteness of the characters of Decimus Brutus and Mark
Antony.

That the author of " Julius Cæsar " had this play in mind
seems natural. Kyd seems, in Malone's opinion at all events,
to have been associated with some of Shakespeare's greatest
plays, and if his drafts of " King Lear " and " Hamlet " were
accepted by Shakespeare as a foundation for his own more
perfect work, we may well believe that he had read and
studied Kyd's " Cornelia " before beginning his " Julius Cæsar,"
more especially as we find the latter play running on exactly
from the point where Kyd's play stopped. In his day Kyd
was held in high estimation. In Mere's " Palladis Tamia " he
is enumerated among the best of the tragic writers of his times ;
and Ben Jonson (" Verses to the Memory of Shakespeare ")
ranks him with Lyly and Marlowe, calling him " Sporting
Kyd." It is not, however, necessary to accept Malone's
theory that Kyd wrote the originals of " King Lear," etc.,
to lend interest to the suggestion here made, that the author of
" Julius Cæsar " had read " Cornelia " before composing his
play, and had consciously and purposely resumed the subject
where Kyd left it. Personally, I should think Malone's suggestion untenable. At the same time, the fact that Shakespeare should have contrived to spin one play on to the web
of another written by Kyd associates the names of the play-
wrights together in a very curious and interesting manner ;
and anything which throws light on the motive and origin of
any of the immortal plays is not only interesting, but profitable
—not only curious, but important.

In taking up an independent examination of any one of Shakespeare's plays, it is always useful and instructive to glance back, in the first instance, at some, at least, of the opinions formed upon it by previous critics. By this exercise the student will find in what a chaotic condition the science of literary criticism has hitherto remained, and the necessity for a more systematic method of appraising the meaning and merits of the author. Above all, he will determine to seek for some canon, or fixed rule, by which to test the truth or failure of his results. The mind of man ever seeks rest in certitude. Mr. Moulton has formulated certain admirable rules of inductive criticism applicable to the plays of Shakespeare, by which we are enabled to take to pieces the mechanism of a play, distribute its parts, and compare them relatively to one another, so as to determine the central idea and the converging lines of action leading to the catastrophe, and thus to get a clear topographical view of the play—the mechanical foundations of the exterior walls, with the internal subdivisions, "staircases, entries, doors, windows, and the like" — plots, counter-plots, under-plots, masques, anti-masques—all harmoniously arranged and distributed in relation to the primary motive of the play, and in illustration of it.

This is a beginning.

Mr. Gerald Massey, also, has recently endeavoured to find some rational centre-point or "axle-tree" around which the Sonnets (so desperately inexplicable hitherto) naturally and

easily revolve. This centre-point he finds—to a great extent—
determined in the fortunes and misfortunes of the Earl of
Southampton, and in the poet's relations to the earl. With
this key to the Sonnets he unlocks the enigmas of each one,
displaying the plain and simple meaning of what before was
dark, obscure, and perplexing. To give an unconditional
sanction to every one of Mr. Massey's speculations is not
required. It is sufficient to appreciate the fact that he has
applied the principles of plain common-sense to the interpretation of the Sonnets, and that his method has proved
eminently fruitful and suggestive. Instead of endeavouring
to imagine a set of circumstances and then fitting the Sonnets
to those circumstances, he has sought to find in the recorded
history of the times the actual facts as they happened, and
by the light of those facts to read the meaning of the Sonnets.
To those of us who are peering back into the vista of the past,
and are trying to get at some clear and rational notion of the
Shakespearian drama—to pierce the mystery of the authorship,
as well as the mystery of the esoteric meaning of much that
was written in that age—and who have taken hold of the
hypothesis that Francis Bacon had a good deal more to do
with the plays of Shakespeare than Shakspere[1] himself—it
will prove no stumbling-block to find that Mr. Massey simply
assumes the existence of a most romantic and chivalrous
attachment between the " glorious vagabond," the actor-
dramatist, and the haughty and impetuous earl. It is always
easy to effect the necessary readjustment of names and matter
to dispel the slight refraction of light caused by Mr. Massey's
primary assumption.[2]

The chief thing is to get a clear notion of what we are about
—to get some fixed standard, some plain groundwork to go
upon. To do this we must begin by removing misconceptions.

Now, if we take any play—say " The Winter's Tale," for in-

---

[1] The Stratford man signed himself "Shakspere." The author is always
" Shakespeare."

[2] There is no record that Shakspere personally ever had the slightest
acquaintance with Southampton. On the other hand, Southampton and
Francis Bacon were close and intimate friends.

stance—and look back to see what the critics have had to say, we find them, as usual, all at sixes and sevens. To start with, they appear (singularly enough) to have entirely misunderstood the motive of the play. Pope even doubted its genuineness. The unities had been so absolutely disregarded—the anachronisms were so glaring—Leontes' jealousy and violence were based upon suggestions so inadequate—the description of Bohemia with a sea-shore was evidence of such ignorance of ordinary geography—the play could not possibly be Shakespeare's. Hazlitt, admitting these defects, apologizes for Shakespeare on the ground he was as likely to fall into " slips " as anybody, " but " (he adds) " we do not know anybody but himself who could produce the beauties." The rest of his study of the play consists of extracts of " beauties," which explain nothing. He points out the saint-like resignation and patient forbearance of Hermione (as if she were intended by the dramatist to represent an ordinary living woman, and nothing more)—the zealous and spirited remonstrances of Paulina—the touching restoration of Hermione to her husband and her child after the long separation of fifteen years. Camillo and the old shepherd and his son are described as " subordinate and not uninteresting instruments in the development of the plot "—and Autolycus is a very pleasant, thriving rogue. Once only does our critic get a faint and accidental glimmering of the truth when he says that we still read the courtship of Florizel and Perdita, *as we welcome the return of the spring*, with the same feelings as ever. To Hazlitt, however, it is " one of the best acting of our author's plays "—and nothing more. The glory and the mystery of the play have entirely escaped him.

The great poet and critic Coleridge is almost as perplexed as Hazlitt, though not so sceptical as Pope. He accepts the play as Shakespeare's, and, while granting that it is exquisitely respondent to its title as a " Winter's Tale," yet it seems to him a mere indolence of the great bard not to have provided in the oracular response (Act II., sc. ii.) some ground for Hermione's seeming death and fifteen years' voluntary concealment.

To him also Hermione is literally a woman, and nothing more. Coleridge imagined that the motive or idea of this drama was a " genuine jealousy of disposition " (which it certainly is not) and that it should be immediately followed by a perusal of " Othello."

This judgment is based on a misapprehension. Othello's jealousy grew out of a thousand and one signs and suggestions leading almost irresistibly to the passion of jealousy. The motive of the play is jealousy. It has no other *raison d'être*. On the other hand, Leontes' jealousy—as Pope shows —is unreasoning and unreasonable, and his fury is unnatural and unreal. This will be seen more fully when we come to analyze the play from our own point of view.

Schlegel treats the play as quite a subordinate one, and devotes less than two pages to a review of it. To him (as to Coleridge), it is a simple tale, peculiarly calculated to beguile the dreary leisure of a long winter evening--hence, a " Winter's Tale." It is a tale of the imagination in which the calculation of probabilities has nothing to do with such wonderful and fleeting adventures. Accordingly, on this ground, he excuses Shakespeare's anachronisms and geographical errors, not to mention other incongruities. The play divides itself (he says), in some degree, into two plays—which he then summarizes — but he misses the symbolical meaning of this division or separation of parts of the play, and he does not know how near the truth he was when he closed his observations with the remark that Perdita seemed to render the rustic feast meet for an assemblage of gods in disguise.

Ulrici, one of the profoundest of Shakespearian critics, devotes several pages to a minute study of " the complicated threads of the dramatic texture " without which he considers the play cannot be understood, and, having unravelled the threads of the texture, he finds that the play is *a picture of life* represented in a strange, cheerful, and eerie manner, a tale told to a circle of poetically disposed listeners gathered round the flickering fireside of a peaceful happy home on a raw winter's night. He notes (but knows not why) that the first three acts are tragical and the last two comic, and he admits that from one point of view the jealousy of Leontes, the conduct of Polixenes, the rescue and recovery of Perdita, etc., appear to be very insufficiently motived. It is surprising that this did not lead the great critic to search for a deeper meaning in the play than appeared on the surface.

As a matter of fact, the play is a NATURE OR SOLAR MYTH, "an allusive or parabolical narration" ("Adv. of Learning"). Looked at in this light, all difficulties disappear; and much of the imagery employed by the poet acquires a fuller and larger meaning, as in truth applying to the tremendous phenomena of nature (objective and spiritual), and not merely to the fleeting incidents of common human life. The scene of the play is laid sometimes in Bohemia, sometimes in Sicilia (Sicily), and this was not accidental. Sicily was an extremely fertile island in the Mediterranean, so fertile, indeed, that it was represented as sacred to Demeter (Ceres) and as the favourite abode of this goddess. Hence it was in this island that her daughter Persephone (Proserpine) was carried away by Pluto. Thus, also, this is the scene of Leontes' kingdom; Perdita's birth; Hermione's trance; of Perdita's restoration; of Hermione's revival; of Florizel's nuptials. In an allegorical play such as this there can be no unities of time or place, and its action should not and could not be identified with any age or place beyond what might be necessary to convey some verisimilitude to human life and fortunes, and to indicate its half-concealed motive. Consequently, whilst Sicily is chosen as the scene for part of the play, owing to its legendary fitness for the subject-matter, and giving the reader a clue to the intention of the dramatist, Bohemia is used as a vague geographical expression, having an impossible sea-shore (as if to impress upon one that the poet did not mean the kingdom of Bohemia in a literal sense), and is used in this general sense for the rest of the action.[1] The anachronisms of time are likewise purposely intro-

---

[1] It may be observed that in the novel ("Pandosta—The Triumph of Time," by Robert Greene) upon which "The Winter's Tale" is founded, the same mistake is made, probably intentionally, as "Pandosta" was clearly an allegorical play, as appears from its very title, which reads as follows, viz. :

duced. Leontes, the king, is somehow suggested by or associated with the city of Leontini, founded in Sicily by the
Greeks, 730 B.C. The Delphic Oracle is consulted, thus throwing the action back to distant and legendary times. In the
same breath we are told that Hermione is the daughter of the
Emperor of Russia, and that Julio Romano (lived 1498-1546)
was the sculptor of the—painted—statue of Hermione.[1] The
unities are disregarded, because there are no unities in Nature
—the anachronisms of place and time are natural; that is to
say, they cease to be anachronisms when Bohemia is understood to be a mere geographical expression, and that one day
is as a thousand in the courts of Nature.

Romano or Pippi was left executor to Raphael, and lived
almost in Shakespeare's time. There can consequently be no
question of any " slip " here. It might be granted that Shakespeare may not have known that Bohemia had no sea-board,
but he certainly knew that Julio Romano did not live in the
days of the Delphic Oracle, consequently Hazlitt's conjecture is
absurd. How do you account for so strange a confusion? The
answer is that Shakespeare felt that the wonderful natural
phenomena he was disclosing by a masque of human life were
not to be identified with any particular time, place or space,
but were to be treated as eternal verities, regardless of those
conditions, and true in the days of the Delphic Oracle as in
those of the Emperor of Russia.

The story reads thus: Polixenes, King of Bohemia, had been
paying a protracted visit of nine months (thereby symbolizing
that the Spring, Summer, and Autumn months had run out) to
Leontes, in Sicily. He desires to return, in order " that no
sneaping winds at home " may blow misfortunes owing to his
long absence. Leontes persuades him to stay longer. Polixenes

---

" Pandosta—The Triumph of Time—Wherein is discovered by a pleasant
history, that although by means of sinister fortune truth may be concealed, it
is most manifestly revealed . . . *Temporis filia veritas* . . . *Omne tulit
punctum qui miscuit utile dulci.*" 1588.

[1] Act V., sc. i., l. 105. Prof. Elze remarks : " He who judges Julio Romano
as correctly as Shakespeare does must have had some knowledge of Raphael,
his master, and of the chief works of the religious pictorial art of Italy."

refusing, Leontes urges Hermione, his wife—identified with Harmony or Nature, the daughter of Mars (War) and Venus (Love) as representing the two opposing forces of Attraction and Repulsion, from which springs harmonious Nature[1]—to prevail with Polixenes. She does so, and thereupon suddenly, without rhyme or reason, Leontes is filled with jealousy of his wife. There is no suggestion of any adequate human motive (as Ulrici admits). If the play, however, be read in a parabolical sense, it was sufficient to indicate that in the course of Nature the Sun yearly turns from his spouse, the Earth.

Camillo, whom Florizel describes as

> " Preserver of my father and of me,
> The medicine of our house !"

is instigated by Leontes to destroy Polixenes. Camillo discloses the jealousy of the king to Polixenes, and they flee the court together to Bohemia.

Polixenes is a more or less shadowy character as a *dramatis persona*, but appears to be a counterpart, for the purposes of the play, of Leontes. There is no special meaning in the speech of Camillo at the opening of the play, except on this hypothesis :

" Sicilia cannot show himself over-kind to Bohemia. They were trained together in their childhood; and there rooted between them then such an affection which cannot choose but branch now. Since their more mature dignities, and royal necessities, made separation of their society, their encounters, though not personal, have been royally attorneyed, with interchange of gifts, letters, loving embassies ; that *they have seemed to be together, though absent ; shook hands, as over a vast ; and embraced, as it were, from the ends of opposed winds.* The heavens continue their loves !

" *Archidamus :* I think there is not in the world malice or matter to alter it."

That is to say, as the season of Winter approaches, Nature

---

[1] Keightley's "Classical Mythology." Hesiod says that Harmonia (Order) was the daughter of Ares and Aphrodite. This has evidently all the appearance of a physical myth, for from love and strife (*i.e.*, Attraction and Repulsion), it is clear, arises the order or *harmony* of the universe.

is, as it were, divided against itself. Nevertheless, there is not, in the world, either malice or matter, in the end and nature of things, to alter the essential relation of the parts to the whole.

> "Hearts remote, yet not asunder,
> Distance, and no space was seen.
>
> *   *   *   *
>
> *Single nature's double name*
> Neither two nor one was called."
>
>   "The Phœnix and the Turtle."

Note also that Polixenes is the father of Florizel (Spring), who becomes ultimately, by his union with Perdita, the heir of Leontes. In ancient mythology the sun is represented under many names as indicating his several attributes.[1] The distraction of Nature is, as it were, indicated in the strife between the sun as Leontes, and the sun as Polixenes, in the rage and fury of Leontes and the flight of Polixenes. Their reconciliation is figured in the union of Perdita, daughter of Leontes, and Florizel, son of Polixenes. Nothing can keep them apart. By the mysterious and everlasting law of Nature, which man defies in vain, Adonis (Florizel) finds Proserpine (Perdita) even in the cold clods of the Earth.

Mr. W. F. C. Wigston[2] points out a similar Dual Unity in Helena and Hermia. The idea (as he points out) is entirely Platonic and abstract, but it would lead us too far afield to follow it up on the present occasion.

We may regard this opening period of the play as equivalent to late Autumn. The Winter is coming on apace. Leontes becomes more incensed than ever with his spouse, and withdraws himself from her completely—casting her into prison, where (like the ripe seed slipping from the bursting pod in Autumn) she is delivered of her daughter Perdita. With the birth of Perdita, Hermione is taken out of the play and remains hidden until the rebirth in the last act of the play.

The king's son and heir, Mamillius, dies of grief at his father's suspicions of his mother's dishonour (Act III., sc. ii.).

---

[1] Sir George Cox says : "Tammuz (or Adonis) became the symbol under which the sun, invoked with a thousand names, has been worshipped."

[2] "Bacon, Shakespeare and the Rosicrucians."

Perdita is repudiated and carried away by the king's order, and thrown down upon the ground somewhere in Bohemia, and is found and taken care of by an old shepherd and his son. These rustic characters represent the clods of Earth in which the seed is deposited to await fructification in the course of Nature. This is the emblem of Proserpine, who was doomed to spend half the year (Winter) with Pluto (the Under-World) and whose rebirth every year corresponded with Spring. On the laying down of Perdita—"the lost one" (Act III., sc. iii.), the ship by which she was carried from Sicily to Bohemia is wrecked and everybody killed or drowned.

The name of Antigonus (who was made by Leontes "the thrower-out" of Perdita) is suggestive of those elements in Nature which may be considered to be in opposition to the everlasting vitality of life in the Universe.

The Winter is now complete. This is shown by the speech of the Mariner, who fears,

> "We have landed in ill time; the skies look grimly,
>   And threaten present blusters. In my conscience,
> The heavens, with that we have in hand, are angry
> And frown upon us."

Antigonus apostrophizes the infant, relates a vision of its mother which had come to him and told him to call the child Perdita; "for the babe is counted lost for ever."

He is destroyed by a bear—also a symbol of Winter and ice-bound regions, the resort of these animals.[1]

This is the tragedy of the first three acts. Hermione, the Earth, has fallen into a trance; Leontes, the Sun, is sad and melancholy, and is without warmth and gladness; Mamillius (the king's son and heir) is dead. Antigonus and all the sailors and persons on the ship who were concerned in the carrying off of Perdita are drowned and killed. The Winter is complete.

To make his meaning clear, and to identify the action of the

---

[1] Mr. Fleay (an orthodox and conscientious Shakespearian of the old school) conjectures that the bear was introduced into this play because it had been a success in "Mucedorus!" To such shifts are the ablest of the Philistines put to account for the most natural and obvious intentions of the dramatist.

drama with the solemn, mysterious, and supernatural, Shakespeare weaves into this part of the play a minor representation which brings us into the presence of the Delphic Oracle—
that divine spokesman of the adamantine Destinies "on whom
heaven, earth, and hell relies" ("Hero and Leander.") Immediately before the swoon of Hermione, and death of
Mamillius, etc., Leontes determined to consult the Oracle, for
which purpose he despatched Cleomenes and Dion to lay the
case before the Oracle, and to bring him the divine message.
The Oracle was as follows: "Hermione is chaste, Polixenes
blameless, Camillo a true subject, Leontes a jealous tyrant, his
innocent babe truly begotten, and the king shall live without
an heir, if that which is lost be not found."

We are permitted to catch a glimpse of the supernatural
in the way in which the Oracle was uttered (Act III., sc. i.).
Cleomenes and Dion are talking together in a street in "some
town" in the sacred island of Sicily where the Oracle was
consulted. Cleomenes praises the climate, the fertility of the
island, and the beautiful temple. Dion replies:

> " I shall report
> . . . the celestial habits
> . . . and the reverence
> Of the grave wearers. Oh, the sacrifice !
> *How ceremonious, solemn, and unearthly,*
> It was in the offering !
>   *Cleomenes.*   But of all, the burst
> And the ear-deafening voice o' the Oracle,
> Kin to Jove's thunder, so surpris'd my sense,
> That I was nothing."

This short and remarkable scene terminates abruptly in the
words of Dion :

> " When the Oracle,
> Thus (by Apollo's great divine seal'd up,)
> Shall the contents discover, something rare,
> Even then, will rush to knowledge.—Go, fresh horses—
> And gracious be the issue !"

The inscrutable laws of Nature work themselves out, and
when the Oracle or Divine Word opens or discovers the
contents of the utterance, then only does the real truth or
knowledge dawn upon our limited human faculties.

Act IV.: Enter *Time*, as chorus. He apologizes for passing over sixteen years since the events of the last act, but he says the result will justify the gap. The scene is now changed from Sicily to Bohemia. We behold Perdita reigning in the nether regions. It is the season of sheep-shearing, and Perdita welcomes the guests to the jollification—amongst whom are Polixenes and Camillo, disguised. To them she presents rosemary and rue,

> " These keep
> Seeming and savour all the winter long :
> Grace and remembrance be to you both,
> And welcome to our shearing."

The Spring has not yet come. Perdita cries :

> " I would I had some flowers o' the spring that might
> Become your time of day ; and yours and yours,
> That wear upon your virgin branches yet
> Your maidenheads growing : O Proserpina,
> For the flowers now, that frighted thou let'st fall
> From Dis's waggon ! daffodils,
> That come before the swallow dares, and take
> The winds of March with beauty ; violets dim,
> But sweeter than the lids of Juno's eyes
> Or Cytherea's breath ; pale primroses,
> That die unmarried, ere they can behold
> Bright Phœbus in his strength—a malady
> Most incident to maids ; bold oxlips and
> The crown imperial ; lilies of all kinds,
> The flower-de-luce being one ! Oh, these I lack,
> To make you garlands of, and my sweet friend,
> To strew him o'er and o'er."

Clearly, we are still in the Winter season. Perdita is still in the courts of Pluto, a spirit governing and managing everything ; " pantler, butler, cook, both dame and servant." As the shepherd says of his old wife (Act IV., sc. iv., 1. 58), she

> " Would sing her song and dance her turn ; now here,
> At upper end o' the table, now i' the middle ;
> On his shoulder, and his ; her face o' fire
> With labour and the thing she took to quench it,
> She would to each one sip."

And thus he bids Perdita play " the hostess of the meeting."
It was the peculiar attribute of Proserpine, that she was called the *Mistress* of Dis or Pluto, an honour (as Bacon

says) not conceded to the wife of any other god; "for the spirit does, in fact, govern and manage everything in those regions without the help of Pluto, who remains stupid and unconscious."

As Bacon's Essay on the subject of the fable of Proserpine may not be readily accessible to everyone, I quote the entire passage. It seems to me to throw a new light on Shakespeare's play of "The Winter's Tale."

"'The fable relates, as I take it, to nature, and explains the source of that rich and fruitful supply of active power subsisting in the under-world and from which all the growths of our upper-world spring, and into which they again return and are restored. By Proserpine the ancients signified *that ethereal spirit* which, having been separated by violence from the upper-globe, is enclosed and imprisoned beneath the Earth (which Earth is represented by Pluto) as was expressed in those lines :

"'Whether that the Earth yet fresh, and from the deeps
Of heaven new-sundered, did some seeds retain,
Some sparks and motions of its kindred sky.'

"This spirit is represented as having been ravished, that is, suddenly and forcibly carried off, by the Earth; because there is no holding it in if it have time and leisure to escape, and the only way to confine and fix it is by sudden pounding and breaking up, just as if you would mix air with water, you can only do it by sudden and rapid agitation; for thus it is we see these bodies united in foam, the air being, as it were, ravished by the water. It is prettily added that Proserpine was carried off while in the act of gathering flowers of Narcissus in the valleys; for Narcissus takes its name from torpor or stupor, and it is only when beginning to curdle, as it were, to gather torpor, that spirit is in the best state to be caught up and carried off by earthly matter. It is right, too, that Proserpine should have that honour, which is not conceded to the wife of any other god, to be called the Mistress of Dis,[1] for the spirit does in fact govern and manage everything in those regions without the help of Pluto, who remains stupid and unconscious."—"De Sapientia Veterum."

---

[1] Act IV., sc. iii., l. 135.

> "*Florizel.*   What you do,
> Still betters what is done. When you speak, sweet,
> I'd have you do it ever; when you sing,
> I'd have you buy and sell so; so give alms;
> Pray so, and for the ordering your affairs,
> To sing them too. When you do dance, I wish you
> A wave on the sea, that you might ever do
> Nothing but that; move still, still so, and own
> No other function; each your doing,
> So singular in each particular,
> Crowns what you are doing in the present deeds,
> *That all your acts are queens.*"

This is the spiritual meaning of the fable—an imprisoned spirit which reigns even in the under-world, and this is the key, also, to the allegorical character of Perdita. She does, in fact, govern and manage everything in those dull regions, among the stupid shepherds and clowns. She is a "changeling" and a princess—the child of Leontes. She

> ". . . smacks of something greater than herself,
>   Too noble for this place."

She is

> "No shepherdess, but Flora
>   Peeping in April's front."

It is she who distributes the flowers and the favours, who dances like the waves of the sea in the sunlight, whose voice is full of the inexpressible charm of living Nature—and around whom the entire action of the play revolves.

Virgil was undoubtedly in Bacon's mind whilst composing the Essay, and (I submit) also whilst composing the play. The sixth book of the Æneid contains a description of the nether regions and of the golden bough hidden in the forest of wood. I quote a few lines from Conington's translation :

> "Deep in a mass of leafy growth,
>   Its stem and foliage golden both,
>   A precious bough there lurks unseen,
>   Held sacred to the infernal queen ;
>   Around it bends the whole dark grove,
>   And hides from view the treasure-trove,
>   Yet none may reach the shades without
>   The passport of that golden sprout :
>   For so has Proserpine decreed
>   That this should be her beauty's meed."

Bacon is perplexed about the spiritual meaning of this precious bough. He says, as for that golden branch, putting aside the explanations of the alchemists, "Here is my opinion of the meaning of that last part of the parable. From many figurative allusions, I am satisfied that the ancients regarded the conservation, and, to a certain extent, the restoration, of natural bodies as a thing not desperate, but rather as abstruse and out of the way, and this is what I take them in the passage before us to mean, by placing this branch in the midst of innumerable other branches of a vast and thick wood. They represented it as *golden* because gold is the emblem of duration, and *grafted*, because the effect in question is to be looked for as the result of art, not of any medicine or method which is simple or natural."

The explanation is somewhat abstruse, but there is a similar passage in the play to the same effect.

ACT IV., Sc. III.

" *Pol.*   'Shepherdess'
(A fair one are you !), well you fit our ages
With flowers of winter.
     Per. Sir, the year growing ancient—
Not yet on summer's death, nor on the birth
Of trembling winter—the fairest flowers o' the season
Are our carnations and streak'd gillyvors,
Which some call nature's bastards ; of that kind
Our rustic garden's barren, and I care not
To get slips of them.
     Pol. Wherefore, gentle maiden,
Do you neglect them ?
     Per. For I have heard it said
There is an art, which, in their piedness, shares
With great creating nature.
     Pol. Say, there be ;
Yet nature is made better by no mean,
But nature makes that mean ; so, o'er that art
Which, you say, adds to nature, is an art
That nature makes. You see, sweet maid, we marry
A gentler scion to the mildest stock ;
And make conceive a bark of baser kind
By bud of nobler race. This is an art
Which does mend nature, change it rather ; but
The art itself is nature.
     Per. So it is.
     Pol. Then make your garden rich in gillyvors,
And do not call them bastards.
     Per.   I'll not put
The dibble in earth to set one slip of them ;
No more than were I painted I would wish
This youth should say, '*twere well*, and only therefore
Desire to breed by me."

Perdita says, in effect, that in her rustic garden, that is in the garden of Nature, she will have no carnations and streaked gillyvors, which some call Nature's bastards. She explains why they are called bastards ; because

> "There is an art, which, in their piedness, shares
> With great creating nature."

The art she refers to is the art of *grafting*. This artificial "improvement" of Nature Perdita contemptuously compares to the tricks of faded beauties, who repair the ravages of time by the aid of the paint-box. She will have none of it, only simple Nature unadorned by artificial means. To this Polixenes objects that by grafting one plant on to another, and so producing another variety of plant, you do not rival Nature, you merely "mend nature, change it rather; the art itself is nature." Thus, as Bacon explains, the golden bough in the forest was represented in the fable as grafted, "because the effect in question is to be looked for as the result of art," something emanating from the intellect, and thus by the aid of Nature "mending" or "changing" Nature. It is a result not springing from accident, not arising "from any medicine or method which is simple or natural."

Bacon, in the "Description of the Intellectual Globe," discusses the question raised by Perdita. He says "it is the fashion to talk as if art were something different from nature . . . .[1] whereas men ought, on the contrary, to have a settled conviction that things artificial differ from things natural, not in form or essence, but only in the efficient; that man has in truth no power over nature except that of motion—power, I say, of putting natural bodies together or separating them— and that the rest is done by nature working within. In one word, the art itself is nature."

Bacon was an accomplished botanist, and wrote a treatise "Of Gardens," which begins with the noble words, "God Almighty first planted a garden. And indeed it is the purest of human pleasures," and so on.

In the royal ordering of gardens, he holds, there ought to be gardens for all the months in the year, and he proceeds to set forth in detail the flowers suitable to be cultivated for every month. Spedding, the learned and accomplished editor of Bacon's works, published in seven stately volumes, points

---

[1] As Perdita, in fact, does.

out that the scene in this play where Perdita presents the
guests with flowers suited to their ages, has some expressions
which, if Bacon's Essay had been contained in the earlier
edition, would have made him suspect that Shakespeare had
been reading it, and he quotes the passage and illustrates it
by a comparison. The theory of the Dual Unity avoids the
difficulty. It cannot be shown that the Stratford Shakspere
knew anything about botany, as there is no evidence that
he ever received even the rudiments of education.

It is a coincidence worth noting that " The Winter's Tale "
was published in the year 1611, and that in that year Bacon
was engaged in the gardens of Gorhambury " experimenting
upon the natures of plants, flowers, and fruits, marshalling
in their proper seasons rosemary and rue, primrose, violets,
cowslips, hyssop, and germande :

> " Hot lavender, mints, savory, marjoram ;
> The marigold, that goes to bed with th' sun,
> And with him rises, weeping ;"

practising the art of grafting and the art of manipulation for
producing new varieties, 'carnations of several stripes,'[1] and
' streak'd gilliflowers ;'[2] trying ' what natures do accomplish
what colours, for by that you shall have light how to induce
colour by producing those natures ;' grafting ' several scions
upon several boughs of a stock ; gathering the excellent dew
of knowledge, distilling and contriving it out of particulars
natural and artificial,' as the flowers of the field and garden."[3]

Shortly before this date (in 1609) Bacon had published his
" De Sapientia Veterum," in which he described the story of
Atalanta as " an excellent allegory, relating to the contest of
Art and Nature, for Art, which is meant by Atalanta, is in itself,
if nothing stand in the way, far swifter than Nature, and, as
we may say, the better runner, and comes sooner to the goal.
For this may be seen in almost everything : You see, that
fruit grows slowly from the kernel, swiftly from the graft ;

---

[1] "Nat. His.," §§ 501, 507, 510.
[2] Act IV., sc. iii.
[3] " Advancement," Book II.

but it is no wonder if Art cannot outstrip Nature, but according to the agreement and condition of the contest, put her to death or destroy her ; but, on the contrary, Art remains subject to Nature, as the wife is subject to the husband."

Now, if it be granted that Perdita is Proserpine in disguise, and that Bacon was the author of the play as well as of the essays which we have quoted, it would be natural for him to introduce this discussion of the effect of grafting—the mending or changing of Nature by means of art or intellect—into the play, as it was one of the mystical incidents which Bacon found underlying the myth, and which he explains in both cases in the same way. On any other hypothesis, the introduction of this incident into the play is unexplainable and without meaning.

But the most interesting feature of this study of the play and comparison with Bacon is (as hinted above) that we find this conception underlying the play, viz., that Perdita represents Proserpine *queening it in the nether regions*, in the time of our winter—a living and active spirit at a time when all seems dead and sapless. This reading brings out the true mythological meaning of the play—the suggestion of an all-pervading spirit — a Pantheistic theory of the universe, such as was held by Bacon. Professor Nichol (ii. 214) says that Telesio's view of the nature of the soul is nearly identical with Bacon's, especially in his holding the *spiritus* that pervades the animal and vegetable world to be a material essence, which in its turn is inspired by a spark of the Divine soul. It is this theory of a universal soul which gives the spiritual colouring to the play, and conveys its true ethical meaning.

As a mere tale it has—as many critics have pointed out—many defects. As a study of human jealousy it cannot be compared to " Othello." Its anachronisms and incongruities, if not intentional, imply an ignorance and stupidity which are incomprehensible. If, however, the play be read as a dramatic representation of the fable of Ceres and Proserpine, all these minor points sink into insignificance. Julio Romano may have painted a picture of Hermione or of Ceres. If so, he would have been bound by no hard and fast rules about period or place, but would have endeavoured to give a representation —or rather *suggestion*—of Nature at large, rather than of any section or part of Nature, and to convey, if possible, an ethical meaning as well as a merely material one. So far from Shakespeare being ignorant of what he was doing in introducing Julio Romano into the play, it has been suggested by Professor Elze that in order to have formed his excellent judgment of this very painter, Shakespeare must have visited Italy. "And whether this hypothesis be accepted or not," he says, "this cannot be denied by anyone acquainted with Shakespeare's works, that his appreciation and judgment of paintings must have been encouraged and developed by re-peated and attentive contemplation of good pictures. . . . The description of the great painting representing the destruction of Troy in 'Lucrece' (lines 1366-1443) is masterly, in spite of some strange bits, as in line 1383 f."

The play, however, is not a geographical or historical lesson; it is not a tale of human passion; it has no elements of love as "Romeo and Juliet" has—of ambition, as "Julius Cæsar" has—of magic, as "The Tempest" has—of debauchery, as "Antony and Cleopatra" has—of vengeance, as "The Mer-chant of Venice" has. Rather, in the spirit of "As You Like It," it is a study of the phenomena of Nature in broad outline —a representation of still life as on the canvas of Julio Romano himself.

Passing from this episode of Perdita playing the queen in the courts of Pluto, we may call attention to another, likewise curious and significant.

In the revels an anti-masque or burlesque[1] is briefly intro-duced.

Three carters, three shepherds, three neatherds, and three swineherds, dressed up in goat-skins, *as satyrs*, are brought

---

[1] ANTI-MASQUE: A grotesque interlude between the acts of *a masque*, to which it serves as a foil, and of which it was at first often a burlesque.— *Murray's Dictionary.*

on the stage, and go through certain antics and then retire. These twelve satyrs symbolize the twelve months of the year, and the four seasons. "Anti-masques," says Bacon, "should not be long, and they 'are usually composed of *satyrs*, baboons, antiques, beasts, etc.'"

It is curious how pat the practice of the poet is to the precepts of the philosopher!

But why should satyrs have been selected for the anti-masque in this particular Nature-play in preference to any of the other creatures used for this purpose? The answer appears to be that satyrs were associated with Dionysius (the Sun-god), and they formed the chorus of the species of drama named from them. Keightley conjectures that it is not un-likely that they are indebted for their deification to the festivals of that god (in which case their introduction in this play would be peculiarly appropriate), and that they were originally nothing more than rustics, who formed the chorus, and danced at them in their goatskin dresses.

On the point of legal knowledge, it may be interesting (by way of addendum) to quote a few instances of familiarity with legal technicalities occurring in "The Winter's Tale" (which play, by the way, is by no means so suggestive in this respect as "Hamlet," and some of the other plays).

To a layman the speech of Hermione (Act I., sc. ii., l. 52)—

> "Force me to keep you as a prisoner,
> Not like a guest ; so you shall pay your fees,
> When you depart, and save your thanks—'

conveys no special meaning.

To the lawyer it recalls an ancient abuse in English law procedure—the dragging back of acquitted prisoners to their cells, in order to satisfy the fees of gaolers.[1] "I remember," writes Lord Campbell, "when the Clerk of Assize and the Clerk of the Peace were entitled to exact their fee from all acquitted prisoners, and were supposed in strictness to have a *lien* on their persons for it. I believe there is now no tribuna England where the practice remains, excepting the two

[1] "Shakespeare as a Lawyer," by F. F. Heard.

Houses of Parliament; but the Lord Chancellor and the
Speaker of the House of Commons still say to prisoners about
to be liberated from the custody of the Black Rod or the
Sergeant-at-Arms, ' You are discharged, *paying your fees* ' "
(compare " The Third Part of Henry VI.," Act IV., sc. vi.,
the scene in the Tower, where Henry inquires of the Lieu-
tenant of the Tower:

> " Master lieutenant, now that God and friends
> Have shaken Edward from the regal seat,
> And turned my captive state to liberty,
> My fear to hope, my sorrows into joys,
> At our enlargement what are now thy fees ?")

Again : it was a custom in olden times, which a lawyer
would be familiar with, that at entering into any contract, or
plighting of troth, the parties clapped (or clasped) hands together
as setting a seal on the transaction.

It is to this custom that Leontes alludes (Act I., sc. ii.,
l. 101):

> " That was when
> Three crabbed months had sour'd themselves to death,
> Ere I could make thee open thy white hand,
> *And clap thyself my love.*"

This was the legal betrothal of Leontes and Hermione, and
symbolizes[1] the breaking up of the three months of the winter
season, and the reconciliation of opposing elements.

Anyone who has read Bacon's " Life and Letters "—and
especially his letters to Queen Elizabeth and James VI.—will
find the exact ring of Bacon's protestations of honest and
faithful service, subject to the infirmities of human nature, in
the words addressed by Camillo to King Leontes (Act I.,
sc. ii., l. 249):

> " My gracious lord,
> I may be negligent, foolish, and fearful ;
> In every one of these no man is free,
> But that his negligence, his folly, fear,
> Among the infinite doings of the world,
> Sometimes puts forth : In your affairs, my lord,

---

[1] " I have heard lawyers say a contract in a chamber, *per verba presenti*, is
absolute marriage."—*Duchess of Malfi.*

> If ever I were wilful-negligent,
> It was my folly ; if industriously
> I played the fool, it was my negligence,
> Not weighing well the end ; if ever fearful
> To do a thing, where I the issue doubted,
> Whereof the execution did cry out
> Against the non-performance, 'twas a fear
> Which oft infects the wisest."

It would take us too far out of the way, and extend this slight essay to too great a length, if I were to seek out parallel passages, or passages containing the exact echo of the above sentiments from Bacon's prose works. By chance I have lighted on a letter addressed by Bacon to the king (1620), in which occurs the following passage, not unlike, in tone and language, to that of Camillo. He thanks the king for certain favours, and adds :

"Then I must say, *quid retribuam?* I have nothing of mine own. That that God hath given me I shall offer and present unto your Majesty, which is care and diligence, and assiduous endeavour, and that which is the chief, *cor unum et viam unum*, hoping that your Majesty will do, as your Superior doth ; that is, that finding my heart upright, you will bear with my other imperfections."

The comparison is apt enough, but search would find many other passages equally, if not more, to the point.

The following passage is instinct with the technicalities of the law (Act II., sc. ii., l. 59) :

> " This child is prisoner to the womb ; and is
> By law and *process* of great nature, thence
> Freed and enfranchised : not a party to
> The anger of the king ; nor guilty of,
> If any be, the trespass of the queen."

" Process " is so called because it proceeds or goes out upon former matter, either original or judicial, and hath two significations : *First*, it is largely taken for all proceedings in any action or prosecution, real or personal, civil or criminal, from the beginning to the end. *Second*, that is termed the process by which a man is called into any temporal court, because it is the beginning or principal part thereof, by which the rest is directed; or, taken strictly, it is the original part of the proceedings (8 Rep. 157).

The indictment of Hermione, in Act III., could only have been drawn by a legal hand.

" HERMIONE, *queen to the worthy Leontes, King Sicilia, thou art accused and arraigned of high treason, in committing adultery with Polixenes, King of Bohemia ; and conspiring with Camillo to take away the life of our sovereign lord the king, thy royal husband ; the pretence whereof by circumstances partly laid open, thou, Hermione, contrary to the faith and allegiance of a true subject, didst counsel and aid them, for their better safety, to fly away by night.*"

The whole scene is cast in a perfectly legal form, and the phraseology throughout is thoroughly legal and technical.[1]

Autolycus, the cunning rogue, has " ribbons of all colours i' the rainbow ; *points, more than all the lawyers in Bohemia can learnedly handle, though they come to him by the gross.*"

The word " point " is used sportively in a double sense. In the technical legal sense it is a distinct position, thesis, or passage in argument, the pith or gist of a legal discussion. In this sense Autolycus could baffle all the lawyers of Bohemia. But the word also means, in referring to ancient costumes, a tagged lace, used to tie together certain parts of the dress. And it is in this sense that Autolycus, the itinerant trader, has such a superfluity. Shakespeare constantly plays and puns with legal expressions in this way.

[1] See " The Law in Shakespeare," by C. K. Davis, pp. 127-132.

London : Elliot Stock, 62, Paternoster Row, E.C.

www.ingramcontent.com/pod-product-compliance
Lightning Source LLC
Chambersburg PA
CBHW030719110426
42739CB00030B/1001